S0-BZK-894

Bridges to the Past

Historic Landmarks of Parke County

By Bob McElwee

Foreword

More than fifty-five years ago, as the summers ended, I would look with great anticipation toward the family pilgrimage to Parke County, Indiana each October.

This three hour trip always began with splashes of color from turning leaves as we drove up and down the valleys. The well maintained gravel roads crossed streams on historic and scenic bridges. Once again we visited mills and dams and walked the sidewalks of towns and villages from another time. Before heading home we bought pumpkins from a small mountain of pumpkins on a farm near Bridgeton and suddenly the outing was over for another year.

Now let's move ahead twenty years, putting World War II behind us and entering the relatively prosperous 1950's. We see Parke County much the same as before, but we can also sense a threat to the historic structures and the natural fabric of the countryside through laissez-faire building and modernization. At this time it is also clear that the county must have an additional economic base besides agriculture. Efforts to bring in large scale industrial developments are unsuccessful.
What, then, can be done?

There were many persons aware of the natural beauty and the historic resources of Parke County. Heretofore, these people simply came at mid-October, traveled the road, enjoyed and went home for another year. Now, a few of these farsighted persons gathered to organize and formalize what had been happening spontaneously. By creating a Covered Bridge Festival, dedicated to the preservation of Parke County bridges, we could share these treasures with visitors. People might come good distances and tourism would be a new element in our economy.

Now let's move ahead thirty-seven more years. The Covered Bridge Festival has been dramatically successful. Despite arson and acts of God the bridges have been preserved, while over one million people visited the county during the 1992 Festival.

New ways were found to broaden the spirit of the Festival. The Maple Fair is held early each year so that visitors can see sugar water taken from trees and boiled at various maple camps to make syrup.

Billie Creek Village was accurately recreated to form a turn-of-the-century settlement where visitors might tread on boardwalks and see the sort of environment their great grandfathers grew up in.

More recently the county has embarked on a program of architectural preservation. The covered bridges are now listed on the National Register of Historic Places while many individual sites are also listed. Bridgeton is our first Historic District on the National Register and Rockville is expected to receive this honor in the near future. This action provides state and federal government recognition of the quality and importance of our historic buildings.

We now come to the purpose of this book. In the thirty-seven years of the Bridge Festival no publication has attempted to combine the beauty, the history and the story of the Covered Bridge Festival and its Parke County heritage. The photography could stand by itself as art, but the captions and the detail bring a sense of place and meaning. We hope this book might bring Parke County to you, or may let you take something of Parke County away with you.

We welcome you to this unique place.

Best wishes,

W. E. Davis

William E. Davis, Registered Architect
Professor Emeritus, Indiana State University
Parke County Historian

Covered bridges – old sheltered trestles
Of hand – hewn, age – burnished beams –
Are like ancient immigrant vessels
Embarked on a voyage of dreams.

Jane. L. Knobloch
7 . 24 . 93

Photo by Allan Miller

Preface

I can remember walking down a country road to the creek to go fishing when I was a boy in central Illinois. The old bridge was wooden, and many of the larger planks were split, offering a view of the water through gaps created by time and by the passing of farm machinery. Now, that bridge has been replaced by a concrete structure to handle larger vehicles. Fishing there would not be the same.

Some of those boyhood memories came back as I walked over the covered bridges in Parke County. On one afternoon in particular, I hiked down a dirt road to take some photographs of one of the bridges. After taking the pictures, I leaned against the railing inside the bridge. The outdoor light was softly filling the far end of the bridge, highlighting the beams that had kept this structure strong for so many years. In the silence of this peaceful moment, I thought I could hear horses and wagons crossing and tried to imagine everything this bridge had been through during the past 100 years.

I have to admire the craftsmanship required to build something that lasts this long...and is still used. I also wonder at the strength of people's fascination with these bridges – their desire to connect with history. These bridges are a part of the past that we want to know more about, a time when life was lived at a slower pace and with different priorities.

One of the reasons I found for exploring the whole county was that it is just plain fun. Besides the bridges, you can walk around the town square, with much of the original architecture still intact. Or, you can have lunch at the Parke County Cafe where the special is a home-cooked meal served with honest hospitality.

Last year I attended the fall Covered Bridge Festival. I found booths and tents with antiques, art and crafts, but no books, calendars or art prints of this beautiful and historic area. Meeting with members of the local preservation group, Parke County Inc., we planned publications that would enable others to enjoy the beauty of this area, as well as raise funds to maintain and restore the bridges. A portion of each publication sale goes toward this restoration effort.

The festival is fun; Parke County is beautiful, but go for the bridges. Opportunities like this are disappearing – America has lost half its covered bridges in the past 20 years. Proverbs 22:28 says it all: "Remove not the ancient landmark which thy fathers have set."

Enjoy the book.

Bob McElwee

Bob McElwee

photo by Gene Howard

Bridges to the Past

Historic Landmarks of Parke County

By Bob McElwee

Photography by Gene Howard, Bob McElwee,
Pat McCarter, and Janean DePlanty

Flying Color Publishing, Champaign, Illinois

Manufactured in the United States of America
Flying Color Graphics, Inc.
This book is printed on acid-free paper.

Library of Congress
Cataloging-in-Publication Data

McElwee, Bob,
Bridges to the Past : photographs by Gene Howard, Pat McCarter, Janean DePlanty and Bob McElwee; foreword by William E. Davis

ISBN 1-884368-00-x

Design by G. Hans Coomer
Composed in Adobe Garamond
Scanning, prepress and printing by
Flying Color Printing & Publishing
Bound by R/R Bindery, Virden, Illinois

Acknowledgements

Our goal at Flying Color Publishing was to produce a book that would give the covered bridge enthusiast a reference guide to the 32 bridges in Parke County. But, we also wanted to give the reader a sense of what the people were like, and a sampling of the historical structures – with a local flavor.

We would like to thank those individuals from Parke County who helped give this book a local touch, making it more than a photo reference book. Their enthusiastic participation has helped to make "Bridges to the Past" a book that is sure to become a collector's item.

We want to thank the Parke County Incorporated (PCI) board for their support throughout the production of all of the publications. Special thanks to Wilbur Engle of PCI, who gives so much of his time to this worthwhile organization, and also for the luncheon meetings at the Parke Cafe.

The office staff at PCI was always there when we needed any kind of information or assistance – thanks to Carolyn McLain and Joyce Wolfe. And, thanks to Jane Vincent in the PCI office, who identified photographs and provided directions for us as we traveled the county.

Anne Lynk, executive secretary of PCI, is the individual in Parke County who had the vision to see that a publication like Bridges to the Past was important, and spent so much of her time working with us at every stage. We also want to thank Anne for her enormous contribution of research for the bridges section of the book.

We want to thank county historian Bill Davis, who provided us with countless hours of his time for the history section, as well as the rest of the book. Bill is one of many Parke County residents who give of their time to help make this area an wonderful place to visit.

Other contributors to the book include Patty O'Neil-Floyd and Marcy Reed who provided research information for the bridges section. Thanks to local poet Jane Knobloch for the poetry that she provided just for this book.

Special thanks to our contributing photographers Anne Lynk, Janean DePlanty, Pat McCarter, Alan Miller and one unknown photographer. We want to thank our featured photographer Gene Howard for his countless trips to Parke County and his excellent photography.

Table of Contents

B.M.

The People of Parke County

Each year people come from all over the world to see the covered bridges of Parke County, Indiana. In October many attend the Parke County Covered Bridge Festival, which features such Midwestern delights as pork chops, bowls of steaming soup beans with cornbread and sliced apples with hot caramel on top. The festival also spotlights local craftspeople, art, and antiques. A walk around the town square lets visitors experience vintage buildings that have been restored in authentic Victorian colors. Maps for driving tours are available to see the covered bridges, or visitors can take guided bus tours during the festival. After leaving Rockville and venturing into the countryside, the rolling hills and winding country roads lead to towns such as Rosedale, Bridgeton, Mansfield or Bloomingdale – all with a past and a story to tell.

The people of Parke County are proud of the bridges and their ability to restore this important part of the area's heritage. Parke County offers friendliness that is genuine and a pace that is relaxing. When people in Parke County say "thank-you," they mean it.

In this section of the book, you can sample the area's natural beauty and take a closer look at some of the people who call Parke County "home."

J.D.

The Covered Bridge Bike Tour provides bikers with the opportunity to enjoy the dogwood and redbud trees as they bloom in the spring. Proceeds from the tour are donated to the Parke County Covered Bridge Repair Fund and local scholarships.

J.D.

Bikers walk across the Billie Creek Bridge at Billie Creek Village.

J.D.

J.D.

Countless country roads wind through
beautiful Parke County.

G.H.

Visitors to the Parke County Covered Bridge Festival purchase tickets for a bus tour of the covered bridges.

J.D.

J.D.

Horse-drawn wagon rides during the Bridge Festival (above). Local chefs prepare for the chicken barbeque (right).

J.D.

Local residents Marvin and Kathryn Hartman have enjoyed many Parke County Covered Bridge Festivals over the years. The festival has grown to become one of the most successful events of this type in the country.

photo by Anne Lynk

J.D.

Soup beans are prepared in large kettles during the Bridge Festival.

The Mushroom Festival is one of the festivals that the community of Mansfield sponsors each year.

P. M.

photo by Anne Lynk

This volunteer is testing out fresh maple syrup during the Maple Syrup Festival, an annual event each March in Parke County.

J. D.

Two visitors to the Bridge Festival prepare for a horse-drawn tour of Rockville.

Mansfield hosts many festivals throughout the year.
Many types of food and crafts are available at these events.

P. M.

J. D.

These young boys eat fresh, hot corn-on-the-cob with their father during the Bridge Festival.

J. D.

These children are playing in the water near the Bridgeton Bridge. Years ago the covered bridge was the center of activity because it was usually located near a mill or town.

Afternoon sunlight filters into the Lieber Memorial Cabin at Turkey Run State Park. The cabin is a memorial to Richard Lieber, "father" of the Indiana park system.

B.M.

G. H.

A cabin stands alone off a
country road near
Turkey Run State Park.

J.D.

A scarecrow contest winner during the
Covered Bridge Festival.

A boy tries his hand at fishing
in a stream near Rockville.

G. H.

The trees begin to blossom on one of the many
scenic country roads in Parke County.

J.D.

G. H.

The Mansfield Roller Mill dates back to 1880.
The mill is a favorite among visitors to the area.

J. P.

Wilma Wooten stirs beans in huge pots
during the Covered Bridge Festival.

J. D.

J. D.

Madonna Dooley stirs the pumpkin butter during the Covered Bridge Festival, while Janet Thomas-Myers makes crafts at one of the many booths. William Helt attracts people to his broom tent with his mongoose.

J. D.

B.M.

The suspension bridge at Turkey Run State Park takes people across Sugar Creek to many of the park's trails and natural wonders.

B.M.

A honeybee is busy at work during the spring.

A boy rests his horse between rides for visitors to the Covered Bridge Festival.

J.D.

A young woman prepares a festival display.

J.D.

J.D.

Linda Schmeltz displays her furs and tanned goods during the fesrtival.

Walking through a covered bridge during the fall.

G. H.

Old wooden, covered bridges transcend
Meandering creeks and streams
Providing a passageway to the past
And the future with present-day dreams.

Jane. L. Knobloch
7 . 24 . 93

G. H.

The West Union Bridge in early autumn.

G.H.

J.D.

A couple enjoys the food available at the festival.

J.D.

Charles Engle makes candied apples during the festival.

B.M.

Bottles of maple syrup glisten in the sun after being bottled during the Maple Syrup Festival in Parke County.

J.D.

Apple slices receive hot caramel from Sue Engle's ladle during the festival.

The Mansfield Bridge is one of the most picturesque on a fall day.

J. D.

The chill of winter brings an icy calm to this scene.

B. M.

G. H.

The changing seasons in
Parke County provide a backdrop
for some of Indiana's most
breath-taking scenery.

A distant view of the Phillips Bridge.

Looking up from a canyon in
Turkey Run State Park.

B. M.

B. M.

A view from the boardwalk
near the general store at Billie Creek
Village, just east of Rockville.

G. H.

The Narrows Bridge on a warm spring day.

An old wagon rests just inside a covered bridge at Billie Creek Village.

B. M.

J. D.

A local vendor sells hams
to festival-goers.

B. M.

A view from the bottom of a
canyon in Turkey Run State Park.

Sun sets on a farm just west of Rockville, with the Phillips Bridge in the foreground.

P. M.

An aerial view of the Mansfield Roller Mill during the Covered Bridge Festival.

G. H.

Mansfield Roller Mill

History

Rich in history, Parke County is blessed to have residents concerned with historic preservation. Not only have 32 bridges been maintained and restored, but many of the structures are in their near original conditions and colors.

Bridgeton is one of two mill towns in the county and is listed as the Bridgeton Historic District on the National Register of Historic Places. The town still has a post office and arts and crafts shops.

Mansfield is another mill town with a working roller mill and covered bridge. Also listed on the National Historic Register, it has arts and crafts stores and annual festivals. Both mill towns provide visitors of today with a glimpse of the past.

Parke County is also home to Billie Creek Village, a recreated turn-of-the-century village with historic buildings and three covered bridges.

Thanks to an active citizenry, Rockville has many sights to capture the eye. The Rockville town square is a required stop for those interested in original architecture and a in chance to see a town square as it was originally built.

A rich past–the area certainly has it. Much of the past has been preserved so that visitors can experience it. The photographs of this section of the book just begin to give an idea of the homes, bridges and buildings that are local, state and national treasures.

J.D.

G. H.

An aerial view of the Rockville courthouse that was built in 1879 and a town square with streets that have original brick paving.

B. M.

Parke County residents who died in the line of duty during World War I are recognized by this monument.

B. M.

This Italian style jail/sheriff's residence was built in 1879. It is located on the southeast corner of the square in Rockville.

G. H.

The Parke Hotel in Rockville (above) was built in 1880 during a flurry of construction that also included the courthouse and sheriff's office.
Most of the buildings on the north side of the Rockville square were lost in the fire of 1871.
Since that time the bottom portions of the storefronts have been altered, but the upper portions are very close to their original design. This corner building (below) remains in its original design.

G. H.

G. H.

The Memorial Presbyterian Church is located on the south-west corner of the Rockville square. Built in 1870, the church boasts an 80 year old pipe organ that is still in use.

G. H.

The Strauss/McCullough bed and breakfast inn, now called "Suits Us", was originally built in 1883. Some of its guests have included Woodrow Wilson, Senator John Kern, Annie Oakley, Irwin S. Cobb and James Whitcomb Riley. This Rockville bed & breakfast inn is one of many in the area, blending history with Hoosier hospitality.

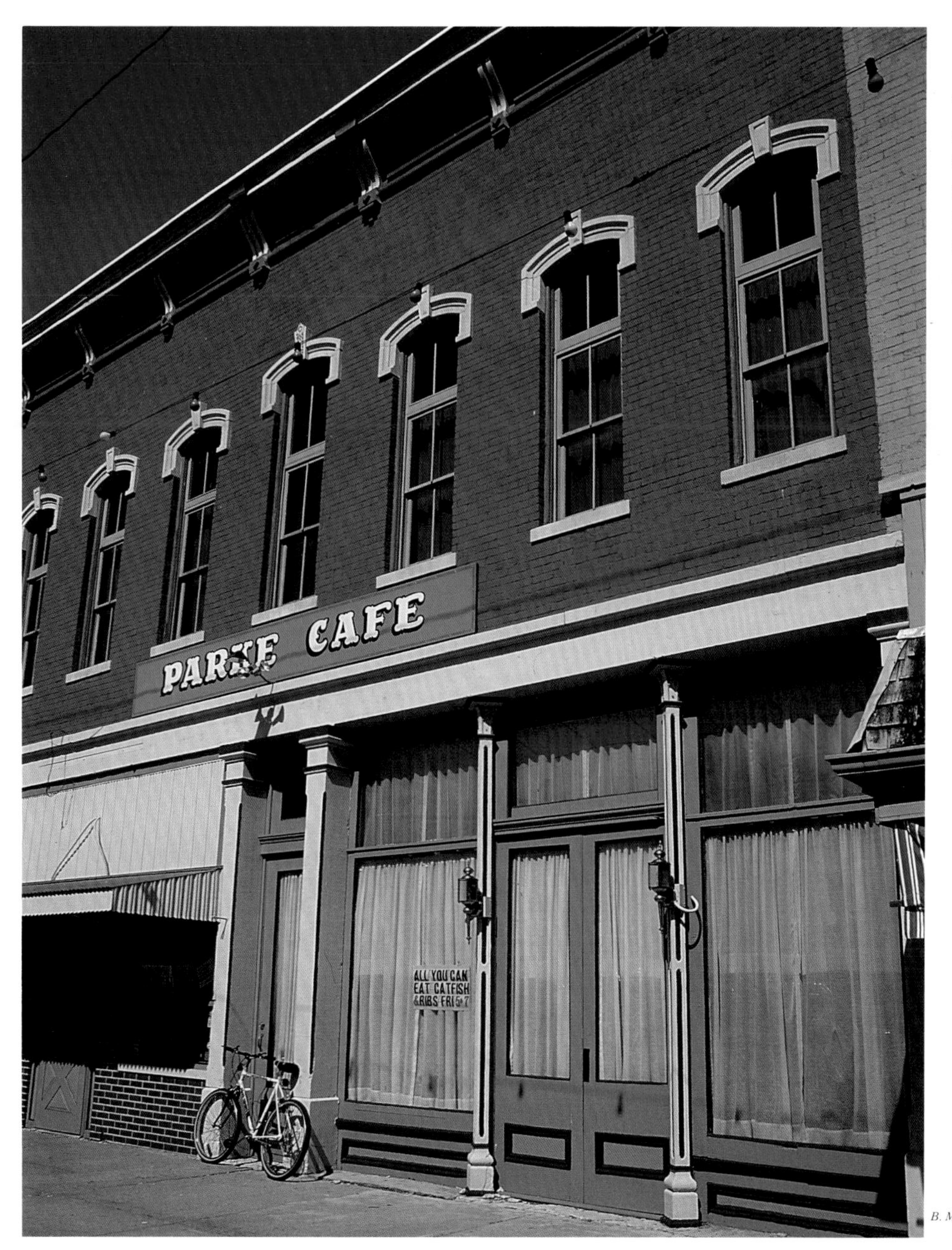

B. M.

The Parke Cafe in Rockville was recently repainted its original colors. The building is located on the east side of the square. Constructed in 1878 in the Italian style of architecture, the building has served as a restaurant for the past 50 years. Visitors can still take a step back in time in this friendly, country restaurant where pies (and most everything else) are still made in their kitchen.

The Friends Church in Bloomingdale was built in 1865 and later received a belltower as an addition. It sits quietly among a grove of beautiful trees in this small town, slightly off the regular tourist trail.

G. H.

G. H.

A winter sunset on the square in Rockville.

Now the Parke County Historical Society and Museum building, this Rockville structure was originally built in the 1830's as a seminary (local high school). During the 1870's a new school was built at a different location, and this building became a school for black children until the 1920's. During the 1930's it was a gas station.

B.M.

The north side of the Rockville square looking to the northeast features the Covered Bridge Art Association Building (tallest).

G. H.

G. H.

The Parke County courthouse is a magnificent structure inside and out. The interior features black & white marble flooring with natural woodwork. The Original Second Empire (French Renaissance Revival architecture) style features a cut limestone roof resting on a sandstone base.

G. H.

G. H.

The Marshall Arch in Marshall, Indiana (top) was built in 1921 by C. Beeson when he was a architectural student at the University of Illinois in Champaign. Built in 1861, Dennis Hall (above) is located in Bloomingdale. When it was in use it was a an agricultural/mechanical school. Later it became a part of the Friends Church.

An aerial view of the Bridgeton area which includes the town, covered bridge and mill.

G.H.

B. M.

The Methodist Church in Bloomingdale is an all-wood structure that was built in the mid-1880's in the Carpenter Gothic style of architecture.

B. M.

A silouhette of a statue on the courthouse lawn in Rockville.

B. M.

This boardwalk in front of the general store is part of Billie Creek Village, a recreated turn-of-the-century village that has 30 historic buildings and three covered bridges. The general store was originally built in Annapolis, Indiana and moved to Bloomingdale following the coming of the railroad about 1874. It was moved to Billie Creek Village in 1968.

The Turkey Run Inn at the Turkey Run State Park is not only a beautiful building, but features a restaurant, lodging and meeting facilities. There are also cabins available.

B. M.

B. M.

This church is now located in Billie Creek Village. Previously it had been a Catholic Church in Rockville, and then moved in the early 1970's to the present location. Many of the original furnishings are still intact including the altar and confessional.

B. M.

This schoolhouse was built in 1913. Located in Billie Creek Village, it is called the Huxford School, originally a public one-room school located north of the Clinton "Y". It was one of the last one-room schools heated by a wood stove.

B. M.

The water makes a whooshing noise as it turns the wheel to grind the grain at the Mansfield roller mill. Visitors can view a mill site that has been operational since 1820. A small gift shop on the lower level offers products from the mill, while browsers out for an afternoon of shopping should enjoy local Mansfield boutiques.

There are several "postcard" views in Mansfield that every photographer should experience. Changes in foliage and temperature are captured in these images, a delightful surrounding for the steadfastness of the roller mill.

G.H.

P.M.

G.H.

G. H.

Bridgeton

Bridgeton is an old mill town in southern Parke County that was first settled in 1816. The Big Raccoon Creek runs through the town and provides water power for the burr-stone grist mill. The grist mill and the area's first saw mill were built in 1823.

Businesses that included a blacksmith shop, a bank, an undertaker, photographer and many others were established during the 1850's. At one time this farming and coal-mining community boasted of a two-story hotel, an opera house and racetrack. While some of these landmarks no longer exist, many have been restored and maintained.

The Weise Mill has been a mill site since 1823. After rebuilding from a fire in 1869, the mill has been the focal point of the community, and is open to the public during the Parke County Covered Bridge Festival in October of each year.

Photos by Bob McElwee

The Bridgeton Covered Bridge pictured above was built in 1868 by J.J. Daniels. It was a working bridge open to public vehicle traffic until 1968. It is now a National Historic Landmark.

Bridgeton offers a variety of shops and businesses, many of which are open only during weekends or special events.

The Mansfield Bridge can be seen through a window in the Roller Mill. The mill is still in operation and open to the public.

B.M.

The train depot in Rockville was built in 1883 on Virginia Street. It was later moved to its present location in 1886. The structure, which is in the Stickstyle architecture, now houses Parke County Incorporated, and serves as the visitor/information center for the county. PCI acquired the building in the early 1970's.

B.M.

A view looking down on the water roller and river from high in the Mansfield Roller Mill.

B.M.

Pumpkins for sale by
a local farmer.

A late evening sun bathes a
country cabin in sunlight.

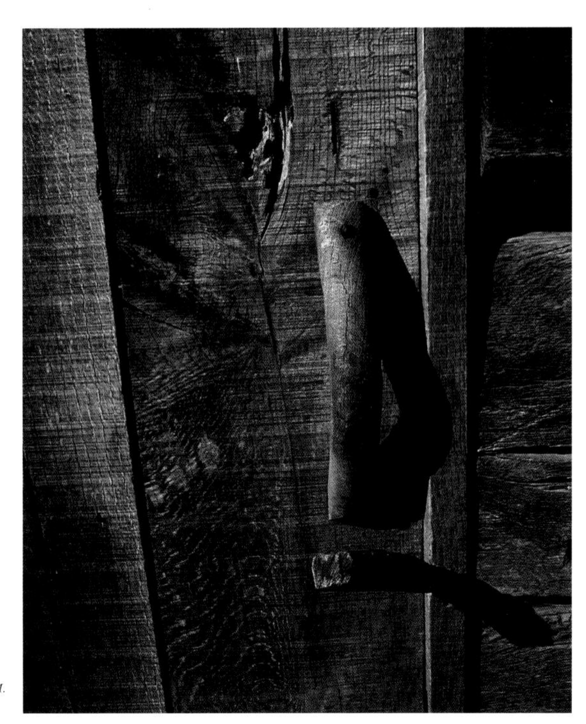

B.M.

Beeson Bridge at Billie Creek Village.

The Bridges

In this chapter, each of the 32 bridges still in existence in Parke County is listed, along with a feature story and photograph of each bridge. Interesting facts such as when the bridge was built, the builder, type of construction and span of the bridge are listed.

The covered bridges of Parke County were built between 1856 and 1920, most of them built by three builders. Including nine others in nearby Putnam County, this area has the largest concentration of covered bridges in the world. Parke County's Covered Bridge Festival draws people from all over the globe. While the number of covered bridges in the United States declines, the popularity of these treasures keeps growing. Indiana's picturesque countryside serves as a perfect backdrop for these links to the past. Fortunately for the public, Parke County's concerned citizens have worked to restore and maintain their bridges. Covered bridges in other parts of the country have not fared as well and are rapidly vanishing.

All of the bridges featured in this section are in existence today, but not all of them are open to vehicle traffic. The only bridge that is not open to the public at all is the State Sanitorium Bridge, which is the only one that sits on private property.

Each bridge has its own unique story. Some people marvel at their architectural design, while others delight in the folklore that surrounds them – the Sim Smith bridge is even alleged to be haunted.

Whatever your interest is, you're sure to find fascinating reading – with local folklore – and beautiful photographs on the following pages.

J.D.

State Sanatorium Bridge

Most often, covered bridges were built for general traffic. The State Sanatorium bridge, however, was built for the sole purpose of hauling coal to the Indiana State Tuberculosis Sanatorium.

On March 8, 1907 the Indiana General Assembly approved the establishment of a state tuberculosis hospital just east of Rockville. Opened in 1910, the Sanatorium was completely self sufficient. A dairy farm, chicken farm, bakery, laundry and power plant provided for three doctors, sixteen nurses and a dentist, as well as the patients.

The Sanatorium was heated and the power plant driven by coal. Coal from mines only one or two miles away from the facility had to be hauled into Rockville, out the State Road (now Highway 36) across the Plank Road covered bridge and into the Sanatorium grounds. A way was needed to cross the Little Raccoon directly into the Sanatorium, so its officials commissioned their own covered bridge to be built.

Parke County's only bridge to have lightning rods was built in 1913 by Joseph A. Britton. Elbridge Boyd used a team of mules to haul material for the concrete foundations and was the first to cross the completed structure. The one span Burr Arch bridge is 154 feet long. The bridge is on private property and is now closed to traffic.

B. M.

Bridge Profile

- Built: 1913
- Builder: Joseph A. Britton
- Construction: Burr Arch
- Foundation: Concrete
- Span: 154 feet
- Creek: Little Raccoon Creek

Portland Mills Bridge

Parke County's second oldest bridge was built across Big Raccoon Creek in 1856 by Henry Wolf. Wolf left his signature in the square portals, characteristic of his building style. The bridge is unique as it is one of only two Parke County bridges with horizontal lapped siding. Burr Arch construction was used for the 130 foot covered bridge.

Unknown

As indicated by its name, the bridge was originally located at the small town of Portland Mills, settled in 1816. Samuel Steele arrived in the town in 1821 and soon established a water powered grain mill and a sawmill for the town. Through the years the mill had a series of owners who made various changes to the building and its machinery.

Portland Mills was destined to be covered with water by the building of the new Raccoon Lake. Moving the covered bridge would serve two purposes. It would save one of Parke County's covered bridges and also the bridge could be used as a replacement for the Dooley Station bridge which had been burned by vandals in 1960. The 18 mile move was completed and the new foundation allowed the bridge to fit into the site of the shorter Dooley Station bridge.

G.H.

The Portland Mills bridge was closed in 1982. A ford is used for crossing the creek. It is in a severely deteriorated condition and local efforts are being made to obtain funding to save the bridge.

Bridge Profile

- Built: 1856
- Builder: Henry Wolf
- Construction: Double Burr Arch
- Foundation: Cut stone moved to poured concrete
- Span: 130 feet
- Creek: Little Raccoon Creek

Mansfield Bridge

The Mansfield bridge, still used by travelers on their way through scenic Parke County, is located in the small village of Mansfield. Nearby is an 1880's roller mill and dam. Constructed forty years after the town was established, this bridge was built under a great deal of public scrutiny. County commissioner Colonel Johnston was elected in 1866, and as some of his staunch opposition had predicted, he soon decided to build a covered bridge. His ethics were questioned because the new bridge was to be constructed between two pieces of property owned by Johnston himself and, in order to access the bridge, a new road would be built on his property.

G.H.

Just one year after his election he commissioned the Mansfield bridge. J. J. Daniels drew up the specifications and it was completed within nine months at a cost of $12,200.00.

The 247 foot Mansfield bridge is a two span Burr Arch bridge. It rests on hewn limestone block abutments and crosses Big Raccoon Creek. Major repairs were done to the abutments, roof and floor in 1980. The Parke County Highway Department replaced the roof and floor again in 1990.

G. H.

Bridge Profile

- Built: 1867
- Builder: Joseph J. Daniels
- Construction: Burr Arch
- Foundation: Hewn limestone block
- Span: 247 feet, 2 span
- Creek: Big Raccoon Creek

Big Rocky Fork Bridge

Named for the creek it spans, Big Rocky Fork bridge is nestled at the bottom of a hill south of Mansfield near the Fallen Rock area. Noted for its deep woods and outcroppings of stone, this rough territory is notorious as a hide-out of the infamous bank robber, John Dillinger.

Adventuresome visitors often climb the rocks nearby to visit the site of a mysterious grave carved out of stone. Several stories are relayed about the origin of the grave. Some attribute its presence to the work of Indians, others to a group of campers in the late 1800's. Most frequently told is the story of Israel Asbury, a local farmer. Asbury is said to have loved the land so dearly that he dug his own grave, an effort to remain on the land throughout eternity. His long toil resulted in a nine foot burial spot, complete with headrest and cover. Alas, poor Israel never achieved his dream. Killed by an oncoming train while resting on a railroad tie, his family buried him in a traditional cemetery.

G.H.

Bridge Profile

- Built: 1900
- Builder: Joseph J. Daniels
- Construction: Burr Arch
- Foundation: Hewn limestone block
- Span: 72 feet
- Creek: Big Rocky Fork

Conley's Ford Bridge

Conley's Ford bridge is constructed with a double Burr Arch, meaning it actually has two arches together. While most of Parke County's covered bridges are built of poplar, this one is of white pine. The bridge is the second longest single span covered bridge still in use and is 192 feet long. It crosses the Big Raccoon Creek between Bridgeton and Mansfield.

J. L. Van Fossen and his father worked for the Parke County Road Department and had experience mostly in building roads and abutments. They had worked with other bridge builders and this solo attempt proved their ability to build bridges as well. The bridge was begun in 1906 and finished in 1907. The construction of this bridge has a marked similarity to the style of J. J. Daniels, one of the builders with whom they worked.

G.H.

Bridge Profile

- Built: 1906-7
- Builder: Jefferson Lawerence Van Fossen
- Construction: Double Burr Arch
- Foundation: Concrete
- Span: 192 feet
- Creek: Big Raccoon Creek

Bridgeton Bridge

G.H.

Bridgeton today has no resemblance to the little town that used to be known as Sodom. Early settlers built its first mill to crack corn for a distillery that was built nearby. With whiskey as its primary product, the area had a reputation for wickedness. Later the town was renamed Bridgeton for its bridge - and probably to help its image.

Earlier open bridges had been built across the Big Raccoon at this site, but both had eventually collapsed into the creek. Bridgeton's picturesque covered bridge was built in 1868. The mill that had been there before had long since burned, the mill that exists now was built the same year as the bridge. The Weise family mill is the oldest continually operating mill west of the Allegheny Mountains.

Probably Parke County's most photographed and painted bridge, the 245 foot bridge is a double span, Burr Arch built by J.J. Daniels. The bridge, towering above the waterfall with the mill in the background, makes a very pleasant composition for any artist's work.

G.H.

At one time, a bandstand stood near the bridge where the Bridgeton Band performed for families on Sunday afternoon. The Bridgeton bridge is still somewhat of a gathering place for local families who come to picnic, swim and climb on the rocks.

Bridge Profile

- Built: 1868
- Builder: Joseph J. Daniels
- Construction: Burr Arch
- Foundation: Sandstone block
- Span: 245 feet, 2 span
- Creek: Big Raccoon Creek

Jeffries Ford Bridge

Jeffries Ford covered bridge is a 204 foot, double span bridge built on the site of the old Jeffries Ford southwest of Bridgeton. This was an ambitious undertaking for bridge builder J. A. Britton. Most of his work had been done on shorter, single span bridges. The length of this bridge required sinking a pier in the center of Big Raccoon Creek to support the bridge. There is now a decided dip in the floor of the bridge due to the settling of the center support.

The building of the Jeffries Ford bridge was a family effort. J. A. Britton was 75 years old and needed the help of his family to do his bridge building. A fortunate man indeed, he was the father of nine sons. The fact that building bridges was a family affair was apparent in a photograph taken at the building site of the Jeffries Ford bridge. Mrs. Britton brought a lunch for the building Britton family and their picture was taken standing on the floor of the bridge before the sides and roof had been built. The efforts of this rather large family resulted in the building of three bridges during the year of 1915.

Recently Jeffries Ford was selected for the filming of a made-for-cable movie by a production group from Chicago.

photo by Lee Merriman

Bridge Profile

- Built: 1915
- Builder: Joseph A. Britton & Sons
- Construction: Burr Arch
- Foundation: Concrete
- Span: 204 feet, 2 span
- Creek: Big Raccoon Creek

Neet Bridge

The Neet covered bridge was built by J. J. Daniels in 1904. This 126 foot burr arch bridge across the Little Raccoon was the last covered bridge built by J. J. Daniels who was 78 years old at the time.

The bridge was originally named for Joe Neet, but members of the Neet family still live in Parke County. Sometimes it is called Dietrich bridge for landowners who lived up the hill from the bridge.

The Neet bridge is on the road from Rockville to Bridgeton and may be one of the county's most heavily traveled covered bridges.

Inside the bridge is a marker noting the repainting of the bridge by Rockville Boy Scout Troop 469. Photographs and paintings done during the last several years show boards in the end knocked out like a smile with a few broken teeth. Recently neighbors of the bridge replaced the ends and repainted them. Taking care of the covered bridges is a labor of love for Parke County folks.

L.M.

Bridge Profile

- Built: 1904
- Builder: Joseph J. Daniels
- Construction: Burr Arch
- Foundation: Concrete, reinforced with wood pilings
- Span: 126 feet
- Creek: Little Raccoon Creek

McAlister Bridge

This 126 foot Burr arch constructed covered bridge was another of the projects completed by builder J. A. Britton. By this time in 1914 he depended primarily on the work of his sons to do his projects as he was 77 years old.

In the tradition of Parke County, this bridge is named after James McAlister who owned the nearby Fairview Hill Farm. The name of the farm was probably selected due to the excellent view afforded by a ridge along the Little Raccoon valley. In the wintertime when the trees are bare, one can see three of Parke County's covered bridges from a vantage point just east of the McAlister covered bridge: Crooks bridge, Neet bridge and McAlister bridge itself.

The raised approaches to the bridge were built to be above the frequent flood waters. This situation was relieved by the construction of Raccoon Lake, built for flood control for the area.

Unknown

Bridge Profile

- Built: 1914
- Builder: Joseph A. Britton
- Construction: Burr Arch
- Foundation: Concrete
- Span: 126 feet
- Creek: Little Raccoon Creek

Crooks Bridge

The Crooks bridge is Parke County's oldest covered bridge. Discussion on building this bridge began in 1850 but construction by Henry Wolf did not begin until 1855. The bridge was then known as the Walker Adams bridge. There has been some confusion about the builder but research indicates that Wolf was the original builder. It was later rebuilt by General Arthur Patterson, whose name is on the bridge's portals. Burr Arch construction was used for the 132 foot bridge across the Little Raccoon.

A portion of the road leading to the bridge was abandoned in 1863 and the bridge was ordered dismantled. Some stories say the creek channel changed and left the bridge over a dry creek bed; others state the bridge was washed to the site in a flood and the bridge was simply jacked up and foundations placed underneath. In any case, until 1867 conflict surrounded the destiny of the bridge. Restoration was only to be done if enough local landowners agreed there was a need for it, but they also had to supply the land for an access road. J. J. Daniels was appointed to select a suitable place for the bridge. He chose the spot known as Darroch's Site, where he felt the bridge would be safe from high water. Although he was commissioned to rebuild the bridge there, no road led to the bridge. The bridge that lay dismantled for four years then remained unused for another thirteen. Sometimes it is called the "Lost Bridge" for obvious reasons.

B.M.

Bridge Profile

- Built: 1856
- Builder: Henry Wolf
- Construction: Double Burr Arch
- Foundation: Hewn stone
- Span: 132 feet
- Creek: Little Raccoon Creek

Catlin Bridge

The Catlin covered bridge was originally located at the north end of Catlin on the road that connected Rockville and Rosedale. Actually a part of the Ben Hur Highway, this was a major route to Crawfordsville. Shortly after Parke County began having the Covered Bridge Festival the bridge was condemned. The bridge was already in poor condition and federal funds were available to improve roads and other bridges. The small Catlin bridge was no longer needed.

Because of the new interest in saving the county's bridges, Parke County citizens raised enough money to move the bridge. In 1961 Bill Diddle Golf Course north of Rockville was selected as the site to place the bridge. Having only enough funds to move the bridge and none left for repairs and foundations, the bridge remained in disrepair on the golf course for a year. Unhappy golfers wanted it torn down. Eventually the bridge was properly set in a new home, repairs were made on the structural parts, and new paint made it a quaint addition to the county's golf course and a pleasing sight to travelers along Highway 41.

G.H.

Bridge Profile

- Built: 1907
- Builder: Clark McDaniel
- Construction: Burr Arch
- Foundation: Poured concrete
- Span: 54 feet
- Creek: Bill Diddle Creek

Nevins Bridge

As the last covered bridge built in Parke County, Nevins bridge was the end of an era. J. A. Britton and his son Eugene built both Britton's and Parke County's last bridge across Little Raccoon Creek. Britton was 83 at the time and died at the age of 91.

The Nevins bridge site has an interesting history of its own. Thomas Gilkerson came from Kentucky in the early 1820's and built a mill and ford here. The small but prospering Gilkerson community was a prospect for the county seat at one time, but Rockville was selected instead. During some difficult financial times, Gilkerson lost the property but then later regained it.

For some time flatboats were built in the town and sent down the Little and Big Raccoon Creeks to the Wabash River.

Thomas Nevins, for whom the bridge is named, bought the Gilkerson property in 1897. Nevins also had interest in mills at Rosedale and Bloomingdale at various times.

Parke County's youngest covered bridge is 155 feet long and of Burr Arch construction with one span. The Brittons used square cut keys, iron straps for reinforcing and iron bracing rods instead of the connecting keys of other bridges.

B.M.

Bridge Profile

- Built: 1920
- Builder: Joseph A. Britton & Son
- Construction: Burr Arch
- Foundation: Concrete
- Span: 155 feet
- Creek: Little Raccoon Creek

Thorpe Ford Bridge

Like many of Parke County's covered bridges, the Thorpe Ford bridge is named for a family that lived nearby. This was previously the site of a ford in Big Raccoon Creek one mile northwest of Rosedale.

The bridge's construction in 1912 can be attributed to the County Commissioner J.M. May. Rather than take the long route from Rosedale to Rockville through Coxville, Commissioner May sought directions for a shorter route. After several periods of being lost, the commissioner vowed a new bridge would be built.

J. A. Britton built this 163 foot bridge on the main route from Terre Haute to Crawfordsville known as the Ben Hur Highway. Elephants and other wild animals were seen traveling the road with the circus on its way to winter in Peru, Indiana.

Even after traffic was diverted to the newly constructed Highway 41 in the 1920's, heavy agricultural use continued across the bridge. Condemned in 1960 and bypassed in 1961, the Thorpe Ford bridge still proved to be a structural phenomenon. The same night in December 1960 that the Dooley Station bridge was burned, all the heavy equipment being used to build the new bypass bridge at Thorpe Ford was taken and parked on the bridge. It is believed that the same vandals were attempting to collapse the bridge. The old wooden covered bridge bore the extreme weight and passed the test of its strength.

G.H.

Bridge Profile

- Built: 1912
- Builder: Joseph A. Britton
- Construction: Double Burr Arch
- Foundation: Concrete
- Span: 163 feet
- Creek: Big Raccoon Creek

Roseville Bridge

More familiarly known as the Coxville bridge, this double span covered bridge is 263 feet long. J. P. Van Fossen (brother of J.L. Van Fossen) built the bridge as a replacement for the bridge across Big Raccoon that had been burned. The original bridge built in 1866 was burned by two men who had been refused service in a saloon because they had already had more than enough to drink. The two angry men left town and burned the bridge behind them.

Roseville/Coxville had a sand plant that crushed sandstone to make glass. They supplied sand to Root Glass Company in Terre Haute, producers of the first Coca Cola bottle. The well known green color of the Coke bottle is due to the content of the Roseville sand.

The small mining town of Coxville became known in later years as the location of the Coxville Tavern. The tavern, now known as the Longbranch Saloon, was owned by the famous bad guy in cowboy movies, Tex Terry.

G.H.

Bridge Profile

- Built: 1910
- Builder: J.P. Van Fossen
- Construction: Burr Arch
- Foundation: Cut Sandstone
- Span: 263 feet, 2 span
- Creek: Big Raccoon Creek

Harry Evans Bridge

Just a half mile north of the Roseville bridge is the picturesque Harry Evans covered bridge. This little bridge is only 65 feet long but makes up for its lack of size with its charm. J. A. Britton built the bridge in 1908 to cross Rock Run Creek. It has the Burr Arch construction and its age is discernable by its modern abutment, concrete.

The road to the bridge has been washed out several times but farmers who live nearby have maintained a ford west of the bridge for years.

The area around Coxville and the Harry Evans bridge is a coal mining area. Several mine shafts are nearby. Rumor has it that one is a "bottomless pit". Bottomless or not, visitors should be aware of the danger of wandering in the unknown territory.

The covered bridge is named for the near neighbor, Harry Evans. However, there is some dispute concerning for which Evans family it was really named. Some area folks deny that Harry Evans lived near the bridge and claim that it was named after another Evans who lived closer. As time passes, the origin of some of Parke County's bridges' names have become more difficult to determine, as stories are most often passed down by word of mouth.

G.H.

Bridge Profile

- Built: 1908
- Builder: Joseph A. Britton
- Construction: Burr Arch
- Foundation: Concrete
- Span: 65 feet
- Creek: Rock Run Creek

Zacke Cox Bridge

The Zacke Cox bridge sits in a secluded area north of Coxville, an ideal spot for photographers and painters. The portal is rather unusual for a Britton-constructed bridge. Recent work was done in the summer of 1992, with extensive repairs that included replacement of the floor.

Named after a prominent family who owned a large amount of property in Parke County, this bridge was built in 1908 by J. A. Britton. He built this bridge at the same time he was working on the Harry Evans covered bridge. Another small bridge, it is only 54 feet long.

Some sources claim that an Indian grave lies between the Zacke Cox and Harry Evans bridges, however, the cliff side has collapsed and now covers the steps and entrance.

Rock Run Creek has uncovered an amazing wealth of fossils for us to study Parke County's pre-historic past. The area near the Zacke Cox bridge has been used as an outdoor classroom for junior archaeologists. In 1956 a large shark fossil was found in the north part of the county, indicating that Parke County was once covered by sea water.

Bridge Profile

- Built: 1908
- Builder: Joseph A. Britton
- Construction: Burr Arch
- Foundation: Concrete
- Span: 54 feet
- Creek: Rock Run Creek

Mecca Bridge

The 150 foot Mecca covered bridge stands at the edge of the small town of Mecca. Although activity is minimal now, the town was once full of thriving businesses. Several coal mines were located here and also the sites of water-powered mills. With coal mines came saloons and stories place the number of saloons in Mecca during the mining era at fifteen or twenty and up to fifty. The Dee Clay Plant offered employment for some three hundred people at one time. They mined clay and manufactured large drainage and sewer tile.

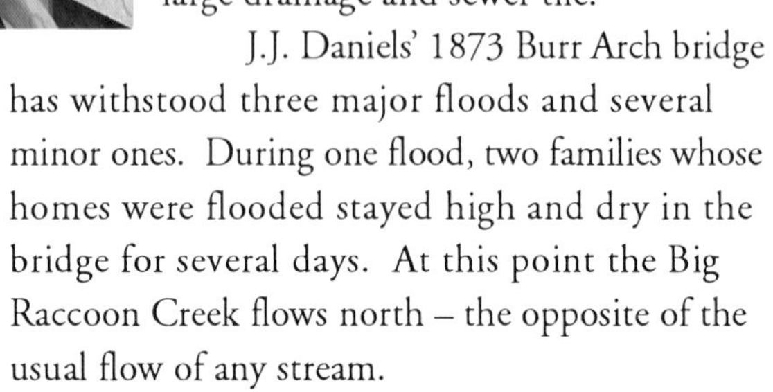

G.H.

J.J. Daniels' 1873 Burr Arch bridge has withstood three major floods and several minor ones. During one flood, two families whose homes were flooded stayed high and dry in the bridge for several days. At this point the Big Raccoon Creek flows north – the opposite of the usual flow of any stream.

At the end of the bridge stands an old one room schoolhouse. This building was bought, moved, and lovingly restored by the active and dedicated Mecca Historical Society. During the Covered Bridge Festival, classes are held here for local school children.

G.H.

Excluding traffic from the bridge has made it available for community activities. Easter sunrise services are held in the bridge. Mecca boasts the only bridge in the county which is fully decorated with Christmas lights during the holidays. Local folks gather to sing and have open house in the one room school. As in the past, the covered bridge remains the center of activity for its local citizens.

Bridge Profile

- Built: 1873
- Builder: Joseph J. Daniels
- Construction: Burr Arch
- Foundation: Hewn Stone
- Span: 150 feet
- Creek: Big Raccoon Creek

Phillips Bridge

The Phillips covered bridge, Parke County's shortest covered bridge, is a mere 43 feet long. (An interesting contrast to the 315 foot West Union bridge). In lieu of the traditional single or double Burr Arch, J.A. Britton used King Post Truss construction. Another Britton King Post bridge, the Weisner bridge, has since been washed away.

Sometimes referred to as the Arabia bridge, the Phillips bridge is located near the area that was known as Little Arabia. It may be that the name resulted from Syrian Moslems who settled near there. Others suggest that the rather unruly folks who lived there were called "Arabians" due to the fact that they were considered to be thugs and petty thieves. The small town of Mecca, which was originally known as Maidstone, may have received its nickname from the same origin. When the people from the Arabia neighborhood came to town, locals were heard to comment rather unkindly that "the Arabs were coming to Mecca".

Not far from the bridge is the Arabia cemetery and the remains of the Arabia church. The number of tombstones in the cemetery bearing the Phillips name suggests the reason for the name of the covered bridge.

B.M.

Bridge Profile

- Built: 1909
- Builder: Joseph A. Britton
- Construction: King Post Truss
- Foundation: Concrete
- Span: 43 feet
- Creek: Big Pond Creek

Sim Smith Bridge

J. A. Britton's 1883 Sim Smith bridge is reputed to be Parke County's only haunted bridge. The road on which it is located was once the main route from Rockville to Montezuma. Highway 36 bypassed this route, but the bridge was saved.

One ghost story tells of a man and his niece on their way to Montezuma and their strange encounter. Upon approaching the bridge the two heard the sound of a horse and buggy coming on the other side. They waited for the buggy to pass through the bridge, but none appeared and the sound faded into the distance. Other travelers claim to have heard the sound and waited, but the buggy has never been seen.

Another story is told that in the mid sixties local teenagers went out at night to investigate the haunted bridge. No sound from a ghost buggy was heard but when they left the car to walk through the bridge, they saw what appeared to be the shadow of an Indian squaw carrying a papoose. In terror, they said they jumped into their car and hightailed it back to Rockville.

The portals of this bridge pose questions of authorship. One end is distinctively Britton's portal, while the other has the portal design most commonly used by J.J. Daniels.

G.H.

Bridge Profile

- Built: 1883
- Builder: Joseph A. Britton
- Construction: Burr Arch
- Foundation: Red sandstone
- Span: 84 feet
- Creek: Leatherwood Creek

Melcher Bridge

The Melcher covered bridge is one of the many Parke County bridges to be known by several names. Sometimes called Leatherwood bridge for the creek it crosses, the Klondyke bridge for a nearby community, it has also been known as the Marion bridge for a local brick factory. The name Melcher was after the Melcher Railroad Station.

The Marion Brick Factory was established at a site east of Montezuma that provided a source of clay for making bricks. Now only a trace of the old gatehouse remains. Business at the factory caused the only Klondyke type of "rush" in the area of the bridge. It was probably built so there would be access to the brick plant from the town of Montezuma.

J. J. Daniels built the 83 foot bridge in 1896. The original foundations are of old type cut stone but in later years concrete was poured around the abutments to reinforce the crumbling stone.

G.H.

Bridge Profile

- Built: 1896
- Builder: Joseph J. Daniels
- Construction: Burr Arch
- Foundation: Hewn limestone and shale with poured concrete
- Span: 83 feet
- Creek: Leatherwood Creek

Leatherwood Station Bridge

The original location of the Leatherwood Station covered bridge was near the Leatherwood Railroad Station. It was during this stop that brick produced at the Marion Brick Plant and other Parke County products were loaded onto the train. Among these products was probably pottery from Samuel Baker's pottery shop where he made redware pottery.

In 1981, the bridge that had cost less than $680 to build was moved to Billie Creek Village at a cost of $42,000. Now it is one of three covered bridges at the Village and is a highlight of the horse drawn wagon ride.

Although J. A. Britton built the bridge in 1899, at some time the Britton portals were changed to a J.J. Daniels arch.

B.M.

Bridge Profile

- Built: 1899
- Builder: Joseph A. Britton
- Construction: Burr Arch
- Foundation: Concrete with original sandstone visible
- Span: 72 feet
- Creek: Williams Creek

West Union Bridge

Parke County's longest covered bridge is a spectacular sight, especially when one considers that it was built in 1876. The bridge is closed to traffic and it is possible to drive the length of the bridge on the modern bypass bridge that runs alongside. Notice should be given to the sandstone center pier that stands in the creek and supports the middle of the double span bridge. It is worth taking the time to park the car and walk the 315 feet across the bridge. The sandy banks of Sugar Creek are a favorite place for both locals and visitors to wade and fish.

County records show that J. J. Daniels built bridges at this location two times before he built the current one. The first bridge lasted five years, the second nine years. His third bridge has been standing the ravages of time and floods for over a hundred years.

G.H.

Bridge Profile

- Built: 1876
- Builder: Joseph J. Daniels
- Construction: Double Burr Arch
- Foundation: Hewn stone
- Span: 315 feet, 2 spans
- Creek: Sugar Creek

Jackson Bridge

A double Burr Arch supports the longest single span covered bridge *still in use.* Jackson bridge is 207 feet long. After building the bridge in 1861 during the Civil War, J.J. Daniels dedicated his bridge to Andrew Jackson. The Jackson bridge is frequently photographed because of its distinctive white color and embellishments in red. Only two of Parke County's covered bridges are white. It is also unique in that it is Parke County's only covered bridge with a cornerstone.

Flatboats were built in several boatyards near the bridge. Local farmers shipped their abundant produce and animals down the creek to the Wabash River and on down the Mississippi River to New Orleans. Boatmen sold their wares and then broke up the boats and sold the lumber. It was a long walk back but many Parke County young men made the trip.

One colorful bridge story is of a local man's memories of taking his grandfather to the bridge to find his name carved on its timbers. When asked about the carving, the grandfather replied that he carved his name on the day the local people hung a Confederate sympathizer in the bridge.

G.H.

G.H.

Bridge Profile

- Built: 1861
- Builder: Joseph J. Daniels
- Construction: Double Burr Arch, double King Post
- Foundation: Hewn stone
- Span: 207 feet
- Creek: Sugar Creek

Marshall Bridge

This pretty little bridge is in an out-of-the-way location crossing Rush Creek. Built in 1917, it is a fairly new bridge for Parke County. It is a 56 foot Burr arch bridge.

There is some question about the origin of the Marshall name. It causes confusion because the bridge is nowhere near the town of Marshall. Some sources suggest that the bridge was named for Mahlon Marshall who served as a Parke County commissioner around 1879 and was a veteran of the Civil War. Others claim the name was for a David Marshall who owned acreage near the bridge.

The Marshall covered bridge was J. A. Britton's next to last bridge building project. He was 80 years old at the time.

G.H.

Bridge Profile

- Built: 1917
- Builder: Joseph A. Britton
- Construction: Burr Arch
- Foundation: Concrete
- Span: 56 feet
- Creek: Rush Creek

Rush Creek Bridge

The Rush Creek bridge was built in 1904 by William Hendricks. Hendricks built only three of Parke County's covered bridges. Fairview Church was just west of the bridge and Church members moved their church away from the creek after it was flooded several times.

The Rush Creek covered bridge is located just south of the small town of Tangier. This uncharacteristic name for an Indiana town was selected by the town's surveyor who had visited Tangier, Morocco. The local post office was opened in 1886 when the town was established and remained open until 1990. In years gone by, the town was a bustling place with several businesses and churches. More recently, however, it has diminished to a tiny community that comes alive during the Covered Bridge Festival with community activities and the scent of Tangier's famous buried roast beef.

G.H.

Bridge Profile

- Built: 1904
- Builder: William Hendricks
- Construction: Burr Arch
- Foundation: Cut Stone
- Span: 77 feet
- Creek: Rush Creek

Mill Creek Bridge

The Mill Creek bridge is another example of how a covered bridge's name changes with the passing of time. The bridge was originally named for Mill Creek, which it spans. It is located on Thompson's Ford so this name was also frequently used. The nearby Wabash River and Erie Canal resulted in the name of the Tow Path Bridge and later it was called Earl Ray bridge, after a well-known auctioneer in the county.

D. M. Brown actually won the contract when the covered bridge was built in 1907. Brown had problems with the construction of the bridge. Perhaps due to his inexperience we don't find his name on other records of bridge building in Parke County. Brown had William Hendricks do the actual bridge construction, but the name on the bridge portals credits D. M. Brown.

B.M.

Bridge Profile

- Built: 1907
- Builder: D. M. Brown, William Hendricks
- Construction: Burr Arch
- Foundation: Concrete, wood, and I-beam supports
- Span: 92 feet
- Creek: (Wabash) Mill Creek

Bowsher Ford Bridge

Several Parke County covered bridges were built in locations where there had been a ford in the stream. Generations of travelers had sought a shallow, flat place in the creek where they could cross. The names of five of the county's covered bridges indicate that fording places were often selected for bridge sites. The Bowsher Ford bridge was built at the ford in Mill Creek that was named after the Bowsher family.

Elmer Garrard had received the contract for the building of the bridge at the Bowsher Ford site but the actual building was done by Eugene Britton. Eugene had learned his bridge building skills from working alongside his brothers for their father. His father was busy building the Jeffries Ford bridge at the time. Eugene was ready to strike out on his own to build the 72 foot Bowsher Ford covered bridge. Visitors will notice that Eugene used his father's trademark Britton portals.

G.H.

Bridge Profile

- Built: 1915
- Builder: Eugene Britton
- Construction: Burr Arch
- Foundation: Concrete
- Span: 72 feet
- Creek: (Wabash) Mill Creek

Coal Creek Bridge

A photograph of the Coal Creek covered bridge is included in our book as a memorial to the loss of this bridge and many other bridges. We are saddened by the destruction of a covered bridge by a storm, flood, or passing of time, but we are appalled and angered by a senseless act of arson. The Coal Creek covered bridge at Lodi was burned by vandals on June 28, 1992. Only one who has stood on the creek bank staring at the charred remains of the bridge can know the feeling of loss to Parke County people, the residents of Lodi in particular.

The original Burr Arch bridge at Lodi was built by J.J. Daniels in 1869. After flood damage in 1898, Daniels rebuilt the bridge. This bridge provided access between the town of Lodi and the rest of Parke County. Lodi was a bustling town during the heyday of the Wabash River and the Erie Canal, however, the last flat boat passed through in 1875.

Enterprising store owners Deverter and Stinebaugh took advantage of the traffic through the bridge by painting signs advertising merchandise for sale at their store. Descendants of Deverter kept the sign repainted for years. Until the bridge was burned, one could read that Deverter and Stinebaugh had both buggy whips and corsets available for sale.

Unknown

Businessmen from Chicago selected the area near an Artesian well in Lodi to develop a health spa. Wealthy visitors would come to the resort area to bathe in the pool of mineral water. A dance pavilion and baseball diamond were on the premises and well-known entertainers performed at shows that were free to guests. Local folks remember Roy Rogers and the Sons of the Pioneers performing there.

Bridge Profile

- Built: 1869
- Builder: Joseph J. Daniels
- Construction: Burr Arch
- Foundation: Stone
- Span: 170 feet
- Creek: Coal Creek

Wilkins Mill Bridge

Grain mills were a hub of activity throughout Parke County. Covered bridges were often built by the mills to provide access to farmers who brought their grain to be ground. Small communities also developed around these areas.

There was a mill near the Wilkins Mill site as early as 1835. It was owned by Solomon Jessup and Zimri Hunt. Zimri Hunt's log barn and house can be seen south of the bridge. George Wilkins bought the mill from the original owner. During Wilkins ownership, he replaced the old mill with a new one that later burned down. That mill was also replaced, existing there until the forties.

William Hendricks built the 102 foot covered bridge that once spanned Sugar Mill Creek. As a result of a flood, the creek changed its course and the bridge is now across a dry creek bed.

G.H.

Bridge Profile

- Built: 1906
- Builder: William Hendricks
- Construction: Burr Arch
- Foundation: Concrete
- Span: 102 feet
- Creek: Sugar Mill Creek (now dry bed)

Cox Ford Bridge.

In 1898 the Parke County Commissioners made a step into the future by having an iron bridge built at the Cox Ford site. The iron bridge stood for a mere fifteen years and was washed out in a flood during 1913.

J. A. Britton contracted to build a new covered bridge as a replacement. The same flood washed out the bridge that Henry Wolf built at Armiesburg. The arches from the Armiesburg bridge were salvaged and used for arches for the new covered bridge at Cox Ford. The old abutments from the iron bridge were raised to protect against flooding.

At the south end of the bridge is an area where visitors can park. The sandy area where canoes land is an ideal spot where the structure underneath the bridge can be viewed.

G.H.

G.H.

Bridge Profile

- Built: 1913
- Builder: Joseph A. Britton
- Construction: Double Burr Arch
- Foundation: Concrete on original hewn stone block
- Span: 176 feet
- Creek: Sugar Creek

Narrows Bridge

The beauty of the Narrows covered bridge, along with the narrows in the rocks, make a scene that is unsurpassed by any other bridge in the Midwest. Artists and photographers frequently select this bridge as their subject for its presentation and also its easy access from the concrete bypass bridge. It is also popular with visitors to Turkey Run State Park.

The 121 foot bridge was built to replace two other bridges built by Salmon Lusk. Lusk's home stands at the top of the hill on the north end of the bridge. It is said that the eccentric Lusk situated his home and the bridge in such a way that he would see all who traveled across the bridge from his house.

This was J. A. Britton's first covered bridge construction project. Those who study the art of bridge construction have criticized his unusual pointed arch joints, but the fact that the bridge remains standing after over one hundred years is proof of the quality of his work.

From the east side of the bypass bridge the place where a millrace and steps were carved out of stone can be seen. This was the site of a mill and pork packaging plant.

G.H.

Bridge Profile

- Built: 1882
- Builder: Joseph A. Britton
- Construction: Burr Arch
- Foundation: Hewn stone
- Span: 121 feet
- Creek: Sugar Creek

Beeson Bridge

The Beeson covered bridge is one of the three covered bridges in Parke County that were built by a professional construction company. Like other bridges, it was named for a family who owned property near its original site north of Marshall.

The Beeson family's 1835 log cabin was moved to Billie Creek Village in 1969. The Beeson bridge was declared unsafe for vehicles in 1969. This and the collapse of another bridge in the area made travel to Marshall, Turkey Run High School and Turkey Run State Park a major problem. An association was formed to find a solution to the problem and during a meeting at Turkey Run High School someone set fire to the bridge. After a second attempt to burn the bridge was made, it was finally moved to Billie Creek Village in 1980 with the moving expenses shared by Parke County Incorporated and Billie Creek Village. The Beeson bridge has now joined the Beeson log cabin and serves as the entrance to Billie Creek Village.

G.H.

Bridge Profile

- Built: 1906
- Builder: Frankfort Construction Co.
- Construction: Burr Arch
- Foundation: Concrete, reset on creosoted wood
- Span: 55 feet
- Creek: Williams Creek

Billie Creek Bridge

The Billie Creek bridge is located on what was the old Plank Road and what later became Highway 36. Like the Sim Smith bridge, it was saved by the re-routing of the highway. J.J. Daniels built the trusses for the 62 foot bridge at his home in Rockville. The trusses were then transported to the bridge site and put in place.

The bridge crosses Williams Creek , providing the nickname Billie for the bridge and the charming recreated turn-of-the-century village surrounding it. In Billie Creek Village visitors can experience what life was like in Parke County at the turn of the century. Two churches, a general store, a one room school, a potter's shop, and a blacksmith shop are just a few of the buildings where craftsmen demonstrate their skills and sell their wares.

G.H.

Bridge Profile

- Built: 1895
- Builder: Joseph J. Daniels
- Construction: Burr Arch
- Foundation: Cut sandstone
- Span: 62 feet
- Creek: Williams Creek

Bibliography

Borum, George. *Guide to the Covered Bridges of Parke County,* 1972.

Hardesty, Barbara. *Welcome to Parke County–A Guide to the Covered Bridge Routes,* 1972.

McCarter, Pat. *The Parke County Guide,* Vol. 6 No. 1, 1993.

Sinclair, Stan. *Illustrated Guide to Parke County Covered Bridges,* 1991.

Snowden, Juliet. *52 1/2 Covered Bridges of Parke County,* 1981.

Weber, Wayne. *The Covered Bridges of Parke County Indiana,* 1980.

J.D.

In today's world of high rise homes and noisy city streets it seems that people reach out for a return to their roots–a remembrance of the past and the value of their heritage. Perhaps this quest is one reason why people return to see and touch Parke County's covered bridges time after time. The bridges stand as monuments to the past and knowing that the bridges stand strong like our time-honored values gives us hope for the future.

Being one of the fortunate people who can walk across a covered bridge where seven generations of my family have trod the same time-worn boards gives me a secure sense of the continuity of life. I bring my granddaughters here so they can know the tranquility I find in the cool shadows of the bridge. Someday these toddlers will bring their children to the bridge.

The stories of the bridges are interwoven with the stories of our lives here in Parke County. We hope that this book will help make a contribution to the preservation of our treasured bridges and others will grow to love them as we do.

Anne H. Lynk

Anne H. Lynk

photo by Tim Hansen

Bob McElwee. *Author and contributing photographer.* McElwee has worked as a photojournalist and as a contributing photographer for over 30 books. Currently, he is the publishing director for Flying Color Printing and Publishing in Champaign, Illinois.

Gene Howard. *Photographer.* Howard provided most of the photographs for the book, including the dust jacket photo. His 40-year career in photography includes 22 years as chief photographer for a daily newspaper and 15 years as a freelance photographer specializing in travel, commercial, and industrial photography. Gene travels with his Siberian Husky, Kiowa (pictured here in Parke County).

Anne Lynk. *Contributing writer, photographer.* The executive secretary of Parke County Incorporated, Lynk provided much of the information and source material for the bridges reference section, as well as festival photographs.

Janean DePlanty. *Contributing photographer.* Deplanty owns and operates two Parke County businesses: Country Shutter Photo Studio and Gobbler's Knob Gift Store.

Pat McCarter. *Contributing photographer.* McCarter is the publisher of the Parke County Guide and co-owner of Greencastle Offset Printing and Graphics.

Patty O'Neil Floyd and Marcy Reed. *Contributing writers to the bridges chapter.*

B.M.

"Remove not the ancient landmark which thy fathers have set."

Proverbs 22:28